2A

Lesson 1

爸爸	bàba	dad	1	姐姐	
妈妈	māma	mum	2	弟弟	
哥哥	gēge	elder brother	3	妹妹	

Lesson 2

床	chuáng	bed	7	桌子	zhuōzi	table	10
柜子	guìzi	cabinet	8	沙发	shāfā	sofa	11
椅子	yǐzi	chair	9	猫	māo	cat	12

Lesson 3

花	huā	flower	13	蝴蝶	húdié	butterfly	16
草	cǎo	grass	14	蜻蜓	qīngtíng	dragonfly	17
鸟	niǎo	bird	15				

Lesson 4

吃	chī	eat	18	面包	miànbāo	bread	22
喝	hē	drink	19	牛奶	niúnǎi	milk	23
果汁	guǒzhī	juice	20	香肠	xiāngcháng	sausage	24
鸡蛋	jīdàn	egg	21	水	shuǐ	water	25

Lesson 5

穿	chuān	wear	26	眼镜	yǎnjìng	glasses	30
戴	dài	wear	27	衣服	yīfu	clothes	31
帽子	màozi	hat	28	围巾	wéijīn	scarf	32
手套	shǒutào	glove	29				

Lesson 6

看	kàn	read, look at	33	画画儿	huàhuàr	draw	38
听	tīng	listen	34	睡觉	shuìjiào	sleep	39
写	xiě	write	35	音乐	yīnyuè	music	40
做	zuò	do, play	36	游戏	yóuxì	game	41
字	zì	character	37				

2B

Lesson 1

春天	chūntiān	spring	42		十一	shíyī	eleven	46
夏天	xiàtiān	summer	43		十二	shí'èr	twelve	47
秋天	qiūtiān	autumn	44		月	yuè	month	48
冬天	dōngtiān	winter	45					

Lesson 2

船	chuán	boat	49		大	dà	big	53
伞	sǎn	umbrella	50		小	xiǎo	small	54
桶	tǒng	barrel	51		两	liǎng	two	55
鱼	yú	fish	52		个	ge	a measure word	56

Lesson 3

胡萝卜	húluóbo	carrot	57		土豆	tǔdòu	potato	60
黄瓜	huángguā	cucumber	58		洋葱	yángcōng	onion	61
青椒	qīngjiāo	green pepper	59		西红柿	xīhóngshì	tomato	62

Lesson 4

晴天	qíngtiān	sunny day	63		下雪	xià xuě	snow	66
阴天	yīntiān	cloudy day	64		闪电	shǎndiàn	lightning	67
下雨	xià yǔ	rain	65		刮风	guā fēng	blow	68

Lesson 5

走	zǒu	walk	69		跑	pǎo	run	72
坐	zuò	sit	70		跳	tiào	jump	73
站	zhàn	stand	71		拍	pāi	pat	74

Lesson 6

娃娃	wáwa	baby	75		气球	qìqiú	balloon	78
蛋糕	dàngāo	cake	76		蜡烛	làzhú	candle	79
风筝	fēngzheng	kite	77		生日快乐	shēngrì kuàilè	happy birthday	80

爸爸

bàba

dad

妈妈

māma

mum

哥哥

gēge

elder brother

Monkey King Chinese School-Age Edition Word Cards 2A−1

3.

姐姐

jiějie

elder sister

Monkey King Chinese School-Age Edition Word Cards **2A–1**

4.

弟弟

dìdi

younger brother

Monkey King Chinese School-Age Edition Word Cards 2A–1

妹妹

mèimei

younger sister

Monkey King Chinese School-Age Edition Word Cards 2A–1

床

chuáng

bed

Monkey King Chinese School-Age Edition Word Cards 2A–2

柜子

guìzi

cabinet

椅子

yǐzi

chair

桌子
zhuōzi

table

沙发

shāfā

sofa

猫

māo

cat

花

huā

flower

Monkey King Chinese School-Age Edition Word Cards **2A–3**

草

cǎo

grass

鸟

niǎo

bird

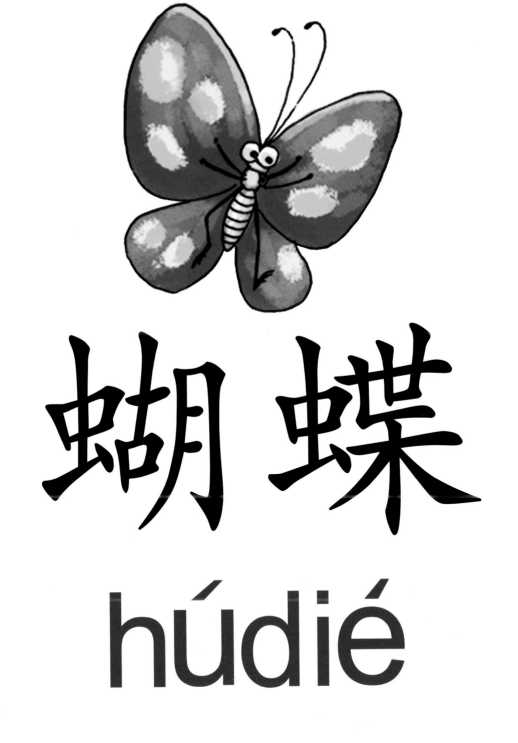

蝴蝶

húdié

16.

butterfly

Monkey King Chinese School-Age Edition Word Cards 2A–3

蜻蜓

qīngtíng

dragonfly

Monkey King Chinese School-Age Edition Word Cards 2A–

吃

chī

eat

喝

hē

drink

果汁

guǒzhī

juice

鸡蛋

jīdàn

egg

面包

miànbāo

bread

Monkey King Chinese School-Age Edition Word Cards 2A–4

牛奶

niúnǎi

milk

香肠

xiāngcháng

sausage

Monkey King Chinese School-Age Edition Word Cards 2A–4

水

shuǐ

water

Monkey King Chinese School-Age Edition Word Cards 2A-4

穿

chuān

wear

戴

dài

wear

Monkey King Chinese School-Age Edition Word Cards 2A–5

帽子

màozi

hat

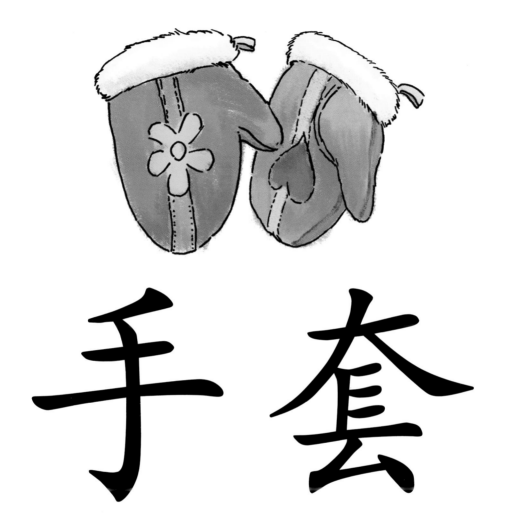

手套

shǒutào

glove

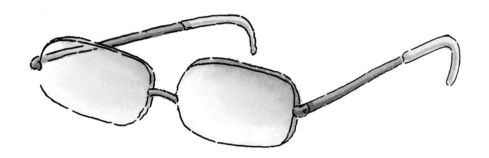

眼镜

yǎnjìng

glasses

Monkey King Chinese School-Age Edition Word Cards 2A–5

衣服

yīfu

clothes

Monkey King Chinese School-Age Edition Word Cards 2A–

围巾

wéijīn

scarf

Monkey King Chinese School-Age Edition Word Cards 2A–5

看

kàn

read,

look at

Monkey King Chinese School-Age Edition Word Cards 2A–6

听

tīng

listen

Monkey King Chinese School-Age Edition Word Cards 2A–6

写

xiě

write

做

zuò

do, play

zì

character

Monkey King Chinese School-Age Edition Word Cards 2A–6

画画儿

huàhuàr

draw

Monkey King Chinese School-Age Edition Word Cards 2A–6

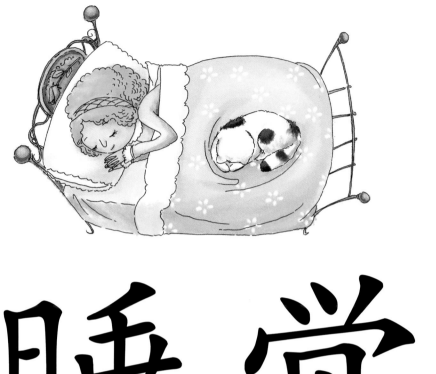

睡觉

shuì jiào

sleep

音乐

yīnyuè

music

Monkey King Chinese School-Age Edition Word Cards **2A–6**

游戏

yóuxì

game

春 天

chūntiān

spring

Monkey King Chinese School-Age Edition Word Cards 2B–1

夏 天

xiàtiān

summer

秋天

qiūtiān

autumn

Monkey King Chinese School-Age Edition Word Cards **2B−1**

冬天

dōngtiān

winter

十一

shíyī

eleven

Monkey King Chinese School-Age Edition Word Cards 2B-1

十二

shí'èr

twelve

Monkey King Chinese School-Age Edition Word Cards 2B–1

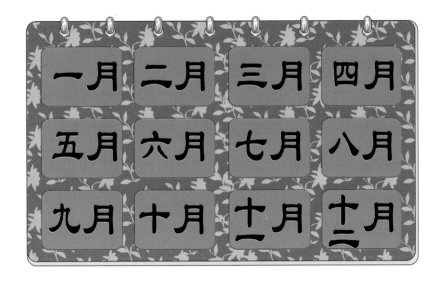

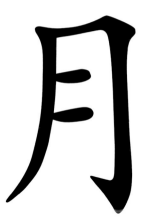

月

yuè

month

船

chuán

boat

伞

sǎn

umbrella

Monkey King Chinese School-Age Edition Word Cards 2B-

桶

tǒng

barrel

鱼

yú

fish

大

dà

big

Monkey King Chinese School-Age Edition Word Cards 2B–

小

xiǎo

small

Monkey King Chinese School-Age Edition Word Cards 2B–2

两

liǎng

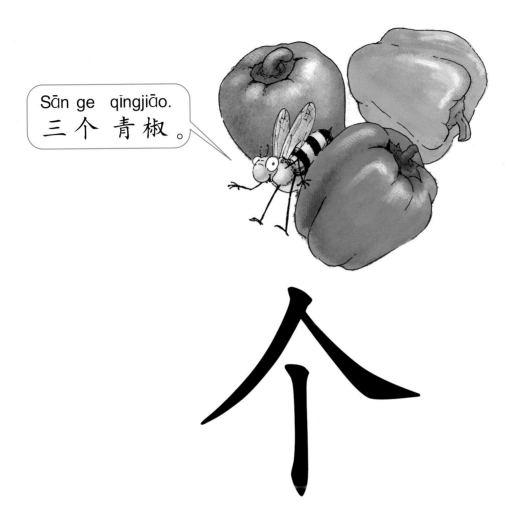

个

ge

a measure word

Monkey King Chinese School-Age Edition Word Cards **2B–2**

胡萝卜

húluóbo

carrot

黄瓜

huángguā

cucumber

Monkey King Chinese School-Age Edition Word Cards 2B—

青椒

qīngjiāo

green pepper

Monkey King Chinese School-Age Edition **W**ord Cards **2B**—

土豆

tǔdòu

potato

Monkey King Chinese School-Age Edition Word Cards 2B-3

洋葱

yángcōng

onion

Monkey King Chinese School-Age Edition Word Cards **2B–3**

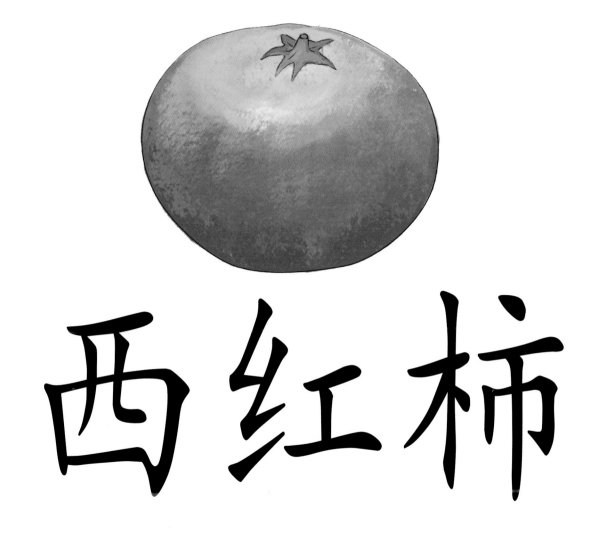

西红柿

xīhóngshì

tomato

晴天

qíngtiān

sunny day

阴天

yīntiān

cloudy day

Monkey King Chinese School-Age Edition Word Cards 2B–

下雨

xià yǔ

rain

Monkey King Chinese School-Age Edition Word Cards 2B—4

下雪

xià xuě

snow

闪电

shǎndiàn

lightning

Monkey King Chinese School-Age Edition Word Cards 2B–4

刮风

guā fēng

blow

Monkey King Chinese School-Age Edition Word Cards **2B–4**

走

zǒu

walk

坐

zuò

sit

站

zhàn

stand

跑

pǎo

run

跳

tiào

jump

拍

pāi

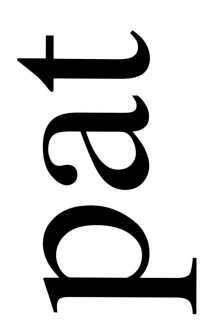

娃娃

wáwa

baby

蛋糕

dàngāo

cake

风筝

fēngzheng

kite

Monkey King Chinese School-Age Edition Word Cards 2B–6

气球

qìqiú

balloon

Monkey King Chinese School-Age Edition Word Cards 2B–6

蜡烛

làzhú

candle

生日快乐

shēngrì kuàilè

happy

birthday

Monkey King Chinese School-Age Edition Word Cards 2B-6